EARLY LIGHTING IN NEW ENGLAND

EARLY LIGHTING

in

NEW ENGLAND

1620-1861

by Helen Brigham Hebard

With sketches by
Ellen Hatch Brewster

CHARLES E. TUTTLE COMPANY
Rutland, Vermont

Published by the
CHARLES E. TUTTLE COMPANY OF RUTLAND, VERMONT
and Tokyo, Japan with editorial offices at
Suido 1-chome, Bunkyo-ku, Tokyo, Japan

Representatives

For Continental Europe:
BOXERBOOKS, INC., Zurich

For the British Isles:
PRENTICE-HALL INTERNATIONAL, INC., London

For Australasia:
BOOK WISE (AUSTRALIA) PTY. LTD.
104-108 Sussex Street, Sydney 2000

Library of Congress Catalog Card No. 64-16175
International Standard Book No. 0-8048-0155-X

First printing, 1964
Fourth printing, 1983

Printed in Japan

Unless otherwise noted, all lighting devices illustrated in the plates are from the Hebard Collection. The approximate date of the three old candlesticks once owned in the Plymouth Colony, described herein, is placed at c. 1650 upon the reliable authority of Prof. Percy Raymond, Past President of the Pewter Club. and that of the Boston Museum of Fine Arts. There is, however, at least some possibility that one of them may indeed have "come over in the Mayflower."

Foreword

Those who have ever heard Helen Hebard present a talk or read a paper on her favorite subject, old lighting devices, before the Rushlight Club or perhaps at a meeting in the House of Seven Gables, can almost hear her speak when they read this book. It is imbued with her pleasant, appreciative personality.

These words of hers were intended to be read at an Antique Collector's Week-End meeting in the village of Sturbridge, Massachusetts. Unfortunately, she was unable to attend because of illness.

Although there are several other books on this subject, each having its own distinctive virtues, none of them make such delightful reading as this, in which the author shares so charmingly with the reader her anxieties and pleasant surprises as a collector.

This is an unpretentious, but at the same time, a highly informative book. It is nicely personalized, but unobtrusively so. It radiates an eager yet restrained enthusiasm. It has an air of spontaneity, and is written in an easy, lucid style. In addition, it occasionally interpolates apt quotations from contemporary sources that give her work the quaint and proper flavor of days gone by.

LEROY THWING

Helen Brigham Hebard
1897-1961

Contents

Introduction

The joy of collecting antiques knows no bounds, for this happy pursuit combines all the pleasures of visiting historical houses, museums and antique shops—not forgetting an auction now and then—with the thrill of discovering an unexpected treasure in the most unlikely spot; and the real satisfaction of finally tracking down that long-sought piece of information after many long hours of research.

As an amateur collector of early lighting equipment my interest far exceeds the scope of my modest collection, or I might add, the limits of my pocketbook. These candles and candleholders, lamps and other lighting accessories I have been gathering over a period of years from many sources, represent many happy hours. Intertwined with the memories of their collecting are vivid recollections of interesting experiences and unforgettable personalities. "Early" is a relative term. People have different conceptions of early illumination. To one person early lighting many mean those nostalgic kerosene lamps of mother's and grandmother's day; to another it may bring to mind some of the primitive clay lamps of the ancient world.

Light has always played an important role in the history of mankind. Its beauty, significance and symbolism, through the ages, constitutes an absorbing study. For unnumbered centuries light has not only served mankind, but it has symbolized its highest aspirations. Like a golden thread we find this symbolism richly woven into the fabric of religion, art and literature. Familiar to us are: Aladdin and his wonderful lamp; the Statue of Liberty, holding aloft her torch of freedom; the classic lamp of learning; Diogenes and his lantern; Lady Macbeth, with her lighted taper signifying the light of conscience; Florence Nightingale with her lamp of mercy; and the lighted candle symbolizing the opposite of darkness, ignorance and evil in the spirit of religious worship.

In the history of this varied and interesting subject the preceding century is actually a part of the modern period of illumination, so let us leave the story of progress in lighting during the last one hundred years to our men of science. Resisting as far as possible the temptation to explore other fields, we shall try to keep within the confines of our topic, *Early Lighting in New England,* and stake out a special claim upon the span of time from the Landing of the Pilgrims in 1620 to the onset of our Civil War in 1861.

From our standpoint, the lights of early New England were feeble and unsatisfactory at best, yet there were at least five means of illumination available to the Pilgrims, Puritans and other early settlers. We shall hope to consider briefly here (1) the log fire, the torch and the spirit light; (2) grease lamps, the crusie and the Betty; (3) the rushlight; (4) candles and candleholders and (5) later oil and fluid lamps—whale oil, lard oil, burning fluid—and Argand type lamps.

Log Fires
Cressets
Torches

Wood as Fuel

Just as the log fire was the first source of light in primitive dwellings where wood was the only fuel, so the hearth fire was an all important and at fist the only means of illumination in the homes of our early settlers. The torch, an offshoot of the fire, could be carried about, thus enlarging man's sphere of activity. Staggering however are the number and variety of torches improvised, fashioned or fabricated for outdoor use. They range from strips of blubber, fat bodies of birds and fish, to dried tree limbs or pine knots. Our pioneers utilized what was available and wood was plentiful in the new land.

The wrought-iron cresset or fire basket was a later development of the above methods. It was used throughout the ancient and medieval periods. In early New England the cresset functioned as special purpose lighting. They were used on fishing boats and for street lighting. An early reference to the blazing beacon on Boston's highest hill gave it its present name—Beacon Hill.

Splint lights are a refinement of the torch used by many people in many places. These slivers of resinous wood are known here as splints or candlewood and in Scotland as fire-candles. They have been used for centuries wherever suitable wood was plentiful. One way of lighting the small homes of northern Europe and the American Colonies, both in the North and the South, was by means of pine splints. Both the Pilgrims and Puritans made use of them, finding in the well-forested new land abundant supplies of resinous wood which was called "candlewood" in the North and "light wood" in the South.

Thin strips or slivers from 8″ to 10″ long were cut from the heart of the fat pitch pine. Candlewood was much used for domestic illumination in pioneer homes. Reverend Francis Higginson of Salem, writing in 1633, describing this candlewood said: "They are such candles as the Indians commonly use, having no other, and they are nothing else but the wood of the pine tree cloven into little slices, something thin, which are so full of moysture of turpentine and pich that they burn as cleare as a torch."

William Wood wrote in his *New England's Prospect*— published in England in 1634: "Out of these pines is gotten the candlewood that is much spoke of, which may serve as a shift among poore folks, but I cannot commend it for singular good, because it droppeth a pitchy kind of substance where it stands."

Govenor John Winthrop, the younger, in a communication to the English Royal Society in 1662 said that candlewood was much used for domestic illumination in Virginia, New York, and New England. It was doubtless gathered everywhere in new settlements.

Pine splints may be carried about in the hands but they are usually burned in a corner of the fireplace where they may be stuck between the bricks or stones of the hearth or placed in a wrought-iron splint holder.

A massive wrought-iron splint holder in the writer's collection is of North European origin. One of these pine splints, timed it at home, will burn about twenty minutes.

Sketches showing type of house built by the Pilgrims in Plymouth, Mass.

Double crusie 1500-1800

Grease Lamps

A shallow iron lamp called a crusie was in use for centuries in Scotland, Ireland and northern Europe. Iron crusies seem to be a more primitive type than the well-developed Roman lamps. During the barbarian invasions and throughout those Dark Ages when the "lamp of learning burned low" these crusies were in use for centuries. Crusies and their descendants, the Betty lamps, were in use on the continent of Europe at the time of the Pilgrims' embarkation. Betty lamps and crusies of northern Europe burned fish-oil or grease, with a rag, reed or twisted flax for a wick.

The first Pilgrim lamp, according to Arthur Hayward, was an iron Betty purchased in Holland by Captain John Carver, first governor of Plymouth Colony, just before he sailed.

Reverend Francis Higginson wrote in 1630 "Though New England has no tallow to make candles of, yet by abundance of fish there of it can afford oil for lamps."

This oil was obtained from the swarms of small fish found in abundance all along the coast. But the light it gave was uncertain, the wick was constantly crusting over and the odor of burning fish-oil was most disagreeable.

Both crusies and Bettys had in common the typical

curved upright band or bail attached at the back of the reservoir, also the hook and spike which make it possible to hang them over the fireplace, or suspend them by driving the spike into the wall. While crusies were shallow open bowl types, Bettys were always covered with hinged or sliding lids. Besides being covered, the Betty lamp had in its oil reservoir a slanting wick-support that made it a cleaner and altogether a "better" lamp, making understandable the accepted derivation of its name.

Occasionaly we find Betty lamps placed upon tin or wooden stands but more frequently they were used about the fireplace. Amazing as it seems today, the Betty lamp was for 300 years the best lighting device in common use. In the South, Betty lamps were used in slave cabins and elsewhere as late as our Civil War.

Rushlight or splint holder with candle socket, shown with burning rushlight.

Rushlight holders

Pricket candlestick

Above: Grisette to hold melted fat through which pith of rushes is drawn to make rushlights. *Below:* Tin Cape Cod spout lamp with cover missing, and a wrought-iron Pennsylvania kettle lamp.

Above: Brass pan type candleholder of the early seventeenth century. *Below:* Turned wooden pickwick and holder, and a tin petticoat lamp with a very rare shield (?) for the flame.

Pewter Ship Anne candlestick, brought over, according to tradition, in 1623 on the ship "Anne." It is seven inches tall and has a
large inch-and-one-quarter socket. Note unusual drip catcher.

Pilgrim Hall, Plymouth, Mass.

Solid brass candlestick of William White, who came over in the Mayflower and was the father of Peregrin White. The candlestick is six inches high. (c. 1650)

Brass candlestick owned, according to tradition, by Gov. Edward
Winslow of the Plymouth Colony. Height: eight inches; diameter
of base: six inches. (c. 1650)

— 25 —

Rushlights

The Rushlight is one of the most intriguing of early lighting devices. Seldom seen outside museums, historical houses and lighting collections, the rushlight consists of a prepared rush clipped into a pliers-like wrought-iron holder. Not only is the rushlight holder a collector's item today, but even rarer, perhaps, is the fragile rushlight itself, prepared in the original manner described in William Cobbett's *Cottage Economy*.

Long before I became interested in early illumination, Rose Briggs of Plymouth had gathered and prepared meadow rushes for lighting. Professor Edwin B. Rollins kept us supplied with fatted rushes for the opening ceremony of the Rushlight Club; he taught me to recognize the lighting rush when growing, as well as to follow the old time method of preparing the rushes.

In my own experiences we have discovered the meadow rush (*Juncu Effusus*) in various places: at Coggswell's Grant, summer home of the Bertram K. Littles in Essex, Massachusetts; along the roadsides and ponds of Watatic Mt.; in the meadows near Lake Winnepesauke, New Hampshire; close to the Kernwood Bridge in Salem and Beverly; on the estate of George W. Price in Peabody, Massachusetts and along highway route 16 in the Ossippe region, where in the late August 1961 the Hebards were parked by the roadside, gathering and peeling rushes.

In the British Isles and possibly in America the meadow rush was gathered in late summer to provide an economical light for the early homes of our forefathers. In England, rushes seem to grow to far greater height and thickness than in America, hence to what extend rushlights were used here in the Colonies is a moot question.

Preparation: After gathering, the rush was first trimmed, then peeled, leaving only a thin supporting strip of green skin. (It is not necessary to soak the rushes provided they are peeled immediately while still fresh and green—good busy work for a summer's evening.) The porous white pith of the rush, after drying, was then drawn through household fat contained in a long, wrought-iron vessel called a "grisset"—one of the rare early utensils.

Use: After seasoning, the fatted rush was placed at an angle in a pliers-like wrought-iron holder, lighted at the upper end and shifted forward as it was consumed. "Lighting the Rush" is a cherished opening ceremony at the Rushlight Club.

Wrought-iron crusie with trammel, 1500-1700

Early Candles

Candles were unknown in Bible days but the candle, in its elementary form, appears in the Roman Era. Pliny, in the First Century AD, refers to Greek and Roman candles of flax threads coated with pitch and/or wax. The candle as we think of it today, however, did not come into general use until the Eleventh Century, according to evidence presented by Leroy Thwing in the *Rushlight*. Thus the true candle in approximately its present form is about one thousand years old. For centuries in the western world tallow and beeswax were the principal substances used for candlemaking. Beeswax furnished the material for ceremonial candles and were made almost exclusively for the Church and nobility. Common candles were made of tallow, and the tallow-dip, made of mutton or beef fat, held its own during the Middle Ages and well into the nineteenth century.

Although accustomed to candlelight in the Old World, Pilgrims, Puritans and early settlers could not use candles freely because they were very scarce and expensive due to the fact that at first there were no domestic animals to supply tallow for candlemaking.

In Bradford's *History of Plymouth Plantation* it is recorded that the first cattle, three heifers and a bull, were brought to this country on the ship "Charity" in 1624. However, it was many years before cattle increased sufficiently to make tallow plentiful. In 1634, John Winthrop, Govornor of Massachusetts Bay Colony, sent over to England for a large supply of wicks and tallow. Candles cost four pence apiece then, which made them costly luxuries for the thrifty colonists.

In addition to the common tallow "dip" made from mutton or beef tallow (preferably a combination of both) and the wax candle, bayberry candles were highly prized by our early settlers. The waxy berries of the bayberry bush found growing in all our colonies provided a natural material for making these choice candles. It had qualities to recommend it, for it would not melt or bend in warm weather, was not greasy to the touch and was fragrant when extinguished. In the fall children gathered the bayberries, which were thrown into boiling water. Since it takes from 4 to 15 pounds of berries, according to credible authority, to make one pound of wax, the work of collecting, boiling and skimming was considerable. Spermaceti candles, aristocrats of the candle family, were made from the waxy solid obtained from the head of the sperm whale.

Candles were first made by the laborious process of hand-dipping—a method which goes back to the Romans and which continued in use in some localities as late as 1880. Candle molding was later introduced by Sieur de Brex of Paris in the fifteenth century. This greatly lessened the work of candlemaking.

Thomas Tusser, in the sixteenth century, wrote in his *Directions to Housewives*:

Wife, make thine own candle
Spare penny to handle.
Provide for thy tallow, e'er frost cometh in
And make thine own candle e'er winter begin."

Mantel in the Hebards' parlor, displaying a three-piece set of gir-
andoles in ormolu and crystal.

Brass and tin, spring type double candle holders with reflectors

Canting lamp (*left*), and two Kinnear patent lamps made by Ufford of Boston.

Sheffield plate candlesticks, eighteenth century

Pan type candleholder (*below*), an eighteenth century candlestick
(*center*), and two rare early seventeenth century candlesticks, all
of brass.

Left to right: a German candleholder, a pair of Benningtonware candlesticks, and a Wedgwood candlestick.

Two hogscraper type candlesticks, a candle snuffer, an extingui-
sher, and a sconce.

Brass candlesticks, including both the piston type and those with side or button candlelifts.

Accordingly, in the early days every thrifty housewife in America saved her penny as in England and made the winter's stock of candles her special autumn household duty —a tedious one at best. Later the housewife was often assisted in her work by the visiting candlemaker who came with his molds and stayed during this arduous undertaking, doing most of those tasks incidental to candle molding. The tallow or wax chandler was the professional candlemaker whose business it was to make candles for sale.

In the eighteenth century a new material, well suited to candlemaking was discovered. Spermaceti, a crystaline substance from the head of the sperm whale, was first introduced into candlemaking in 1750. Spermaceti candles are associated with exciting tales of the whale fishery of New England—a story of romance and adventure fraught with danger and hardships, yet an enterprise which brought independence to many New England families and wealth to the communities carrying on the whale-fishing. Sperm whales differ from whalebone whales in having teeth and an enormous development of the upper part of the head, which is about as large as one half of the body and serves as a float to raise the nostril above the water. In this large head are cavities containing a light oil, which is all liquid during the life of the animal, but which after death solidifies into a granular yellow substance—crude spermaceti—and exudes the permanently liquid sperm oil. The upper part of the head near the nostril, called "the case," contains the most solid spermaceti; the lower portion or "junk," more of the sperm oil. After a whale was captured it was brought alongside the vessel, the head was severed and hoisted to deck level. Then began the first duty to bale out the case.

This crude material is separated by filtrations and pressings and purified by chemical treatment. In its pure state, spermaceti is unfit for candlemaking as it assumes a decidedly crystalline structure on cooling, and it is rather brittle. This is corrected by adding to it five to ten percent of wax, the mixture being cast in molds.

Spermaceti is highly prized for candlemaking on account of its elegant, pearly, translucent appearance and the purity of the light. It proved to be superior even to the candles made of wax and gave more light than tallow candles. Spermaceti candles were a standard measure of artificial light. The term so often used—one "candle-power"—is the light given by a pure spermaceti candle weighing one-sixth of a pound, burning at the rate of 120 grains per hour. In 1750 Benjamin Crabb was granted the exclusive privilege of manufacturing sperm candles in Massachusetts for fourteen years. Soon these candles were among the standard commodities shipped in New England trading schooners to the southern colonies and West Indies. By 1761 there were eight sperm candle factories in New England and one in Philadelphia. (This description is taken in part from a treatise on *Oils and Candles* by W. Matheiu Williams, published in 1876.)

In 1845, it was written in Thomas Webster's *Encyclopedia of Domestic Economy* that "candles supply the most convenient and the most general mode of obtaining artificial light for domestic purposes. Until lately two substances only, wax and tallow, were known as materials for candles; spermaceti was next introduced, and at present (1845) various substances such as stearine, etc. are added."

The next advance after spermaceti was the manufacture of stearine fat from which the smoky, smelly glycerin has been extracted. Without going into the technical details we may say that if fat be exposed to considerable cold and pressure, the stearine will remain. Thus, from Chevreul's discovery and researches up to 1823, improvements by M. de Milly in 1855 and by Twitchell in recent times stearine was found to be a material better adapted than tallow for candlemaking. Stearine burns with a clear, smokeless flame, does not "gutter" and is particularly suited for tropical use because it does not bend when exposed to warmth.

Pan type brass candleholder, seventeenth century

Brass candlestick owned by Gov. Brewster of the Plymouth Colony c.1650

Candleholders

The candle is a very adaptable light source. It may be and often was burned with only the hand as holder, as beautifully illustrated in a seventeenth century French painting by Georges de la Tour entitled "The Education of the Virgin" (Frink Collection, N. Y. C.).

In Pilgrim Hall, Plymouth, you can see the William White brass candlestick brought over on the Mayflower in 1620. Cast of solid brass like other seventeenth century brass candlesticks of the period, it is short, measuring only six inches in height, with a grease cup or drip pan at the base of the voluted stem.

In the development of the candleholder, the drip pan was gradually moved up until in the latter half of the sixteen hundreds it was found midway on the baluster type stem. The two in our collection are not a pair—one has a four-inch, the other a five-inch drip pan—the turnings are also different. One was purchased at an auction gallery on Boylston Street, Boston, the other in a Third Avenue antique shop, New York City. This castle, or mansion type, is more frequently seen in Williamsburg, Virginia. Hanging in the Worcester Art Museum, the Dutch masterpiece painting of "A Woman Praying" by Nicholas Maes, 1632-1693, serves to identify this candleholder and date it about 1650.

Household articles of brass were brought to the Colonies from England and the Continent. Very little brass work was done in America prior to the end of the 18th Century. Brass is an alloy of copper with zinc, and zinc was not commercially mined in this country until 1837.

One of our joys in collecting is a brass skillet candleholder found on a junk table in a New Hampshire antique shop. This brass saucepan or skillet candleholder is a Dutch type. A similar candleholder was discovered among the ruins when the site of the First Trading Post of Plymouth Colony in Aptuxet was excavated and is now displayed there in the restoration. There the Pilgrims and Dutch met for trading at Bourne on Cape Cod. This skillet candleholder was identified by Pieter De Hooch's Dutch painting of "The Mother" dated about 1650, which formerly hung in the Berlin Art Gallery and which was displayed here in 1949.

Solid cast brass or wrought-iron candleholders were superceded by hollow stem candlesticks about 1710. They were called "sliding" candleholders on account of the rod with thumb piece or knob used to raise the candle.

Sheet iron sliding candlesticks according to Lindsay's *Iron and Brass Implements of England and America* were not commonly used until the early eighteen hundreds. To be complete they should have a spur-like hook at the rim. In addition, the thumb piece for lifting the candle was often impressed with the name of the ironmonger. Uncovered beneath the rust and paint are often found good old names such as Sargent or Pollard. You all are doubtless familiar with the stories told about these utilitarian iron candleholders. Always turn a hollow stem candle stick upside down to see if the push-up is there—intact. (Frankly I am not sold on this so-called improvement for I have never been able to operate it smoothly. It usually sticks, or shoots the candle out like a rocket.)

C. Malcolm Watkins in his Smithsonian Institution *Report on Artificial Lighting in America 1830-1860*, calls attention to the two contrasting worlds. The scale of living differed in backward areas from that of the cultural centers and this duality of standards was reflected in the lighting facilities. Not only was there wide divergence between the humble dwellings and the homes of the well-to-do, but even in the same household great contrast was evident.

In the American Colonies in the latter part of the seventeenth century candles were luxuries. Candlewood, fire lights, grease lamps and log fires continued to furnish light in kitchens and humbler dwellings, but candles illuminated the drawing rooms of grander homes. Small tables made in the gate-leg and trestle types served as candle stands. In the eighteenth century candles were in more general use and American candlestands with Chippendale and Sheraton lines were probably made in goodly numbers. In days when conversation and cards constituted the evening's amusements, many of the card tables were provided with round flat places on which to stand the candlesticks.

Candles were burned in many other interesting utensils such as lanterns, sconces, wall brackets and chandeliers of varied designs and materials. Candleholders have been made of utilitarian wood, iron and tin; lustrous pewter and shining silver; gleaming brass, sturdy pottery, sparkling glass and delicate porcelain, representing many stages of culture and craftmanship and affording the collector of early lighting devices a fascinating field for research as well as a never-ending source of pleasure.

The candle "student lamp" c. 1820 is one of my favorite candleholders. We believe these were made by American manufacturers. Wallace Nutting's *Furniture Treasury*, volume II, plate 4116, shows an identical candle holder discribed as follows: "Square iron standard on a weighted tin base. Candlesticks and hoods in tin, formerly the author's."

In Arthur Hayward's *Colonial Lighting* plate 40, a single candleholder is described as follows: "A very quaint and unusual specimen, the property of the Worcester Historical Society. This they call an upright candle student lamp. The stand and shade of tin and very well done, both the shade and candleholder being adjustable on the square center rod which terminates in a brass ring for carrying. The rod starts from a deep saucer base, which is weighted with sand so that it is not easily tipped over. The curved arm which supports the candleholder is very prettily made. This was used by Elijah Demond while he was a student at Dartmouth College and Andover Seminary from 1816 to 1820." Thus the date of a "candle lamp" of this type is generally conceded to be about 1820. The story of acquisition by exchange and authentication of the writer's lamp is recorded in *The Rushlight* for November, 1958. We also have a three-piece girandole mantle set of ormolu and crystal c. 1840.

It is a pleasure to use early lamps and candleholders in furnishing one's home, especially when they are decorative. Some have an acanthus leaf motif and were in vogue when three-piece candle and lamp sets were accepted mantle garnitures in the 1840's. In the late nineteen-forties, whenever I was in Boston I would walk by a certain antique shop to reassure myself that one of these coveted candelabra sets was still in the window. Finally I succumbed and brought it back to Plymouth and later to Salem where we have treasured it ever since as tangible evidence of John Keat's famous line: "A thing of beauty is a joy forever."

The spring candlestick appears to be very old and was

Above: Brass lard or sperm oil lamps. *Below:* Lard oil lamps with very wide wicks.

Above: Free blown glass lamps with cork disc burners, commonly known as "courting" or "sparking" lamps. *Below:* Glass lamps, two with blown fonts and pressed glass bases, and one a blown glass peg lamp. Two of the three have cork disc burners and the third a screw-in burner.

Sinumbra lamp with New England Glass Company base

Light bronze, gilded solar type astral lamp

Candlestand with shades and candle bracket adjustable for height

Bronze Argand lamp with astral type burner and combined chimney and shade (c. 1840).

Bronze astral lamp with original glass

Left: Incomplete burner from a lamp by the New England Glass Company. *Right:* Sinumbra lamp by W. Carleton of Boston, showing ring shaped oil font.

probably in use as early as 1660. However, records show that about 1845 an Englishman named Palmer made improvements on candles and candlesticks, his device being a spring placed in the tubular stem. The candle was thrust down the tube, compressing the spring, and was held by a locking cap which held the upper end of the candle. The candle was forced up by the spring as it burned, so there was no excess as it dripped. We may place most of these spring candleholders in the middle part of the last century, although they continued to be made and used long after that.

Two pulpit lights having the spring feature in the stems were given to me—one an outstanding act of generosity, the other an unexpected surprise. When visiting friends in Ashby, Massachusetts, we were taken up Watatic Mountain to look at a lovely old hilltop house which they were eager to have us buy. We were charmed with the house and surroundings. The house had been unoccupied for a number of years and as I peered in the windows I discovered that a few pieces of furniture had been abandoned. I saw an old rocking chair and on the floor, half hidden behind it, a pulpit light. We did not buy the house but later friends acquired the property and made a special trip to Plymouth to present me with the lamp.

The pierced tin lantern of colonial days is really only a covered-in candleholder. When the candle is lighted, the lantern casts a lovely lacy pattern of light and shadow upon ceiling and walls. Its constantly flickering candle flame sheds a wavering light that adds mystery to the dim delicacy of its design—a quality entirely lost if the lantern is electrified. I like to imagine it placed in a dim shed or hung in the shadowy hallway of an early American home.

Pickwick and pewter lard oil lamp with flat burner c. 1845

Whale and Lard Oil Lamps
Pegs and Petticoats
New and Better Burners

Oil and Fluid Lamps

We must retrace our steps to resume the story of the lamp. Following our War for Independence there were a number of developments which revolutionized illumination. They were: the flat wick burner invented by M. Lequs of Paris in 1783; Aime Argand's central draft burner and glass chimney; Englishman John Miles' patent in 1787, which effected the upright wick tube and gave us the closed-in reservoir or font from which was derived our typical whale oil lamp; lard oil lamp burner patents granted over a thirty year period from 1833 to 1863; and the camphene or fluid lamps introduced about 1840.

The whale oil lamp represented a great improvement in lighting, although the use of grease and fish oil lamps continued, since there was always an overlapping of types in use. Whales were found in large numbers off the shores of New England and a well entablished whale fishery was underway here by the latter part of the seventeenth century. In 1671 Nantucket, under its old name of Sherburne, was the greatest whaling town in the world. And from the port of New Bedford whaling vessels put out to sea for more than 200 years (1680-1880). We think of the whale oil lamp, especially, in connection with the period following our Revolutionary War—in the days of our growing prosperity and expansion westward—when the clipper ships and the great whale fishing fleet brought romance, adventure and wealth to New England.

Common whale oil lamps are of a distinctive type; they are upright, having a closed top reservoir and a central vertical wick tube. On account of the heavy nature of the oil, the wick tube extends well down into the reservoir but is short above the lamp. An earlier type of whale oil burner was the cork-disc burner. The round tin wick tube was inserted through a cork which was capped with a tin disc. Stamped on the small tin disc one may discern the word PATENT which is believed to date about 1810. An original whale oil lamp with its cork disc burner is increasingly difficult to find because in time the cork dries out, causing it to shrink, fit more and more loosely into the neck of the lamp, and frequently to be discarded.

A choice pair of wine-glass courting lamps c. 1820 would be fitted with their original whale oil cork-disc burners. When the daughter of the house entertained her gentlemen friends, the tiny flames of these whale oil courting lamps doubtless gave sufficient light to cover the conventions, yet not enough to prove embarrassing. On special occassions, such as Valentine's Day, we like to burn sperm whale oil in one of these tiny courting lamps.

Also in our collection is a small glass lamp with waterfall base and blown font and a clear blown-molded peg lamp, both having their original whale-oil cork-disc burners.

The peg lamp is unique because it was the first all-glass lamp to be made in America.

It is also unique because it was designed to be set into a candleholder. It is another example of the never-ending need for economy. The peg or socket lamp could be carried about from room to room and then placed in a stationary position in a candle socket anywhere to give light for any purpose.

To quote Lura Woodside Watkins—"The earliest document thus far discovered that points unquestionably to the familiar glass whale-oil lamp is a New England Glass Company bill of sale, dated May 1, 1822, which lists '3 doz. peg lamps' at six dollars." Peg or socket lamps were used until after the Civil War and are dated by style, shape, and type of burner. The first example was probably plain blown and was fitted with a cork-disc burner.

A later development of the early whale-oil burner introduced in 1830, was the type where the burner was threaded to screw into a metal collar on the lamp—known as the screw thread burner.

The petticoat lamp has a skirt added to the peg, making it a quaint and versatile lighting device. It can be placed in a candle socket, carried about or stood on its own base on a table. An addition to these examples of Yankee ingenuity is a solid brass bonnet-like top attached by a chain to its screw-thread burner, for use, possibly, as a shield.

Tin, pewter, brass and glass whale oil lamps utilized the screw-thread burner after 1830. Of these, brass lamps are by far the most rare. In our collection are two pairs of brass table lamps, one having egg-shape fonts with single wick-tube screw-thread burners; the other having acorn-shape fonts with double wick tubes.

The pair of glass whale oil table lamps in the collection may be described in terms of the glass collector as "waisted loop font, high dome top and hexagonal standard, made by the New England Glass Company, about 1847" but they will always be associated with the memory of a perfect summer day in New Hampshire. The shady country roads were dappled with morning sunshine. In the distance, deep blue mountain ranges were outlined against the clear blue sky and soft white clouds. High up in the little village of Sandwich, New Hampshire, we chanced upon a beautiful old house with antique shop adjoining. There it was with its gorgeous view of range upon range of mountains—like a gem in a perfect setting. And there it was that these whale oil lamps were bought.

The search for a cheaper lighting fuel led to the introduction of lard oil in New England as early as 1820. Lard oil was a heavy, yellowish fluid, a by-product of the process of lard-making. It was cheaper than whale oil and burned with a steady, fairly bright flame.

New fuel oils when available were burned in old lamps. Gradually new burners better adapted to them were developed and patented. In order to overcome the drawbacks of heaviness and the tendency to thicken in cold weather, lard oil burners were evolved with a broad flat wick. Between the years 1833 and 1863, fifty patents were granted for lard oil lamps. Their purpose was usually to provide some method of heating the oil.

The two pewter lard oil lamps in our collection are good examples of excellent quality and pleasing design. The broad flat wick holder made of copper for good conduction of heat, extends far down into the heavy fuel oil.

Another style of lard oil lamp is the Ufford patent of 1851 which may not be handsome, but represents the last word in the ordinary lighting of its day. It is a combination of iron and tin, having its original gilt lacquer; it has the typical broad flat wick; and is equipped with matching smoke shade set above the flames.

A tin lard oil canting lamp with reflector is made of tin, brass, iron and copper. It was originally lacquered with peacock blue glaze some of which still remains on the back of the reflector. The canting reservoir designed to utilize every last drop of oil makes this lamp a most ingenious, economical and interesting lighting device. This resembles one of a pair of lard oil lamps used by Noah Webster when compiling his dictionary published 1836. (See illustration in Arthor Hayward's *Colonial Lighting*.)

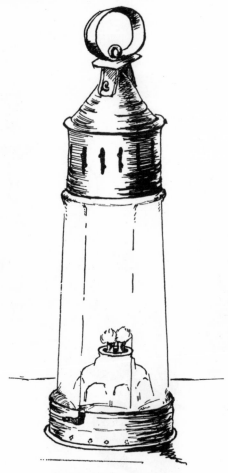

Tin lantern 1820-1840

Free blown glass lamp with drop burner c. 1820

Argand-Type Burners

Introduced in 1834, burning fluids like Porter's burning fluid consisted of refined turpentine with the addition of alcohol. They were highly explosive, when burned in old lamps, often with tragic results, and were accepted only with great apprehension. About 1840 a new burner was introduced, designed especially for this highly explosive fluid. It has tall tapered wick tubes of brass—all above the fluid. If complete it will come equipped with wicktube caps attached to the burner in order to contain an unpleasant order and to prevent evaporation of the fluid.

A glass, burning fluid tavern lamp of Star and Punty pattern is a prize. It is complete with its two wick-tube caps attached, and is perfect in every way. Its Sandwich glass pattern makes it a collector's item, if for no other reason. Its generous size is an appealing feature, too. Fortunate indeed was the tavern guest who drew such a lamp to light himself to bed. One could read until the wee small hours of the morning by the light of its two flames.

Although the first Argand lamps in this country burned sperm oil, patents utilizing the Argand principle were taken out for lard oil and camphene as well. Variations on the Argand principle were found in the mantel arm type. In the solar lamp designed to burn lard oil, the flame is drawn up through a central hole in a convex metal disc above the burner, into a tall column of light. The sinumbra type astral has a ring-shaped reservoir. By the 1840's many of these handsome lamps were imported or even manufactured in this country for use in the better homes. There were lovely table-type hanging lamps and mantel sets of silver, brass and bronze with glass shades and prisms. Thus for whale, lard and sperm oil lamps, the Argand principle was important.

Name plates usually appear on Argand Lamps but often they seem to complicate and confuse. The name on the plate may be that of the patent owner, the manufacturer, the seller or the maker and dealer combined.

In Pilgrim Hall, Plymouth, there are two side lights of a three-piece mantel set used on the pulpit of the Church of the Pilgrimage in 1840 at the dedication of its new edifice. They are marked:

Alfred Wells
& Co.
Boston

Alfred Wells was listed in the Boston Directory as a merchant.

And in the home of Mrs. George S. Parkers, Essex Street, Salem, Massachusetts is an Argand lamp labelled:

Messenger & Sons
63 Hallon Garden
London & Birmingham
Manufactured for
Alfred Wells
Boston

The two-branch bronze mantel lamp in the writer's collection has printed on the name plate:

Messenger & Sons
London and Birmingham
Manufactured for
Jones, Low and Ball
Boston

Jones, Low & Ball was the firm name in 1839 of the present Shreve Crump & Low Company, Inc.

The brass hanging Argand type astral lamp in the writer's collection is labelled on the burner stem:

Manufactured by
H. N. Hooper
Boston

H. N. Hooper won a gold medal for his exhibit of lamps listed in the catalogue of the Massachusetts Mechanics' Association First Exhibition and Fair in 1817.

One of our most exciting finds was an Argand astral-type hanging lamp. About three years ago we made a special trip to Winterthur to study their Argand lamps in order to complete a paper on "The Argand Lamp in America." We returned full of information but without any Argand Lamps. We drove back to Boston on a chill, gray afternoon in late November. My husband suggested a detour through Lowell Street near the North Station. This dismal street was lined on both sides with decrepit old buildings, housing antique shops—a place that a woman would not care to go unaccompanied.

As we came near the end of this dubious street, I thought I recognized a lighting device hanging from the ceiling of a dusty shop window, so we went in to look at it. It looked original but we could not be sure, so asked the dealer if it was a marked piece. He offered to check, placed a high step ladder in the window and climbed up to examine the lamp with a flash light. My husband and I looked expectantly upward while the rumpled but obliging dealer peered intently at the lamp, aided by flash light and magnifying glass, while my husband steadied the ladder.

Almost too good to be true, the lamp was marked on the burner stem **H. N. Hooper,** one of the foremost manufactures of Argand lamps in Boston. Although electrified it was undamaged and was equipped with its original cut and frosted glass shade. I longed to acquire it, and an indulgent Santa Claus gave it to me for Christmas. It has hung ever since in our Salem home.

Continuing its influence over more than a century, the Argand central draft principle was adapted to the gas lamp and to Argand-type kerosene burners. The kerosene student lamp, popular from 1875 to 1900, was not only an adaptation of his principle but almost a copy of Argand's original lamp.

Petroleum and Kerosene: Following whale oil, lard oil and burning fluid, a new fuel for the lamps of America was discovered. Colonial E. L. Drake studied the possible relation of geological formations in Pennsylvania to pools of underground oil and decided that petroleum could be obtained by drilling. In 1859 he backed his convictions by drilling the first oil well in America. Later kerosene was distilled from petroleum. Soon new coal oil burners appeared, but it was not until after our Civil War that the kerosene lamp was used to any great extent. Then many of the lovely old whale oil and fluid lamps were fitted with kerosene burners. Many of them now are being electrified for use in this twentieth century.

It burns like a torch and makes a terrific smoke. And we can testifiy to Wood's statement of long ago that "it droppeth a pitchy kind of substance where it stands."

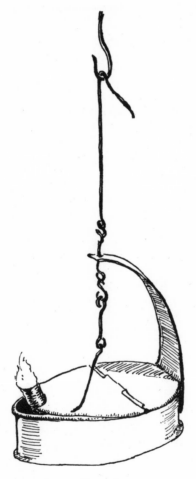

Copper Betty lamp

Conclusion

Most of us have struggled through several New England hurricanes and blizzards by the light of oil lamps or candles, hence we realize that it is a far cry from the fragile rush-light and tallow-dip to our modern, machine-molded candles, and that there is little resemblance between the smoky, smelly Betty lamp of our forefathers, or even the handsome whale oil lamp, and the brilliant electric lamp of our twentieth century.

We depend upon the candle when the lights go out. Considering simplicity, cleanliness and portability, the candle is a remarkable light source. Candleholders of rare craftmanship and beauty are among our most treasured possessions and on our most significant occasions we enjoy the loveliness of candlelight. Of all forms of lighting known to the Old World as well as to the modern period, the candle holds first place for grace and charm. Who can deny that the lamp and the candle have lighted the path of progress and that they symbolize all that is finest and best in our civilization today.

Argand wall and table lamps. Note unusual draft cone on lamp in center photo.

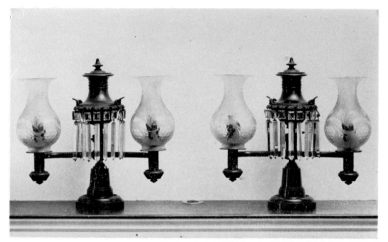

Double arm Argand mantel lamps

One of a pair of Argand mantel lamps with marble ormolu base and crystal drops.

Early form of student lamp (c. 1860)

Brass sinumbra lamps with original glass

Hall lamp

Argand sinumbra type hall lamp by Hooper & Co., Boston. Mentioned in text on page 67.

Bronze Argand mantel lamp, probably the middle lamp of a set of three.

Early Lighting Accessories

The story of Early Lighting would not be complete without a list of lighting accessories, any one of which is a noteworthy subject in itself:

Candle rods
Candle molds
Snuffers—for trimming candle wicks
Candle boxes—for storing candles
Save-alls—thrifty devices consisting of a base and pins
    to utilize the last bits of tallow
Extinguishers—for putting out candles
Flint and tinder boxes
Matches, first slender strips of wood, dipped in sulphur,
    used to carry the flame from the tinder to the
    candle or kindling
Early sulphur matches—1827
Oil fillers
Spill holders
Wick picks

Two accessories I would like to comment on briefly: candle snuffers and wick picks. Candle snuffers, scissors-like accessories, were used to trim the charred end of a candle wick, which was called "snuff." Have you ever tried to snuff a candle? Only a clumsy performance would result in extinguishing the flame while trimming the wick. For putting out candles there are special cone-shaped extinguishers. Candle snuffers were made obsolete when the early, twisted cotton was superseded by the self-consuming plaited wick, invented by Combaceres in 1825.

The wick pick was useful for adjusting the flame of a whale oil lamp. As the wick burned it required raising and trimming. The size of the flame was increased by raising the wick, or decreased by lowering it. That was accomplished by inserting the pick into the side slot of the whale oil wick tube.

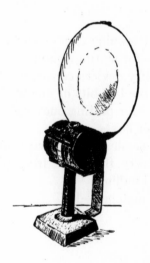

Tin canting lamp 1840-1850

Bibliography

Ashley, Clifford W.—*Yankee Whaler*
Ashton, John—*Dawn of the XIX Century in England*
Ashton, John—*Social Life in the Reign of Queen Anne*
Brand, John—*Popular Antiquities,* Vol. 3
Clifford, C. R.—*Junk Snupper*
Cobbett, William—*Cottage Economy*
Dexter, George Blake—*Lure of Amateur Collecting*
Earle, Alice Morse—*Home Life in Colonial Days*
Encyclopaedia Brittanica—Article on "Candlemas"
Encyclopedia of Domestic Economy
Freeman, Larry—*Light on old Lamps*
Gould, Mr. and Mrs. G. Glen—*Period Lighting Fixtures*
Hadley, Grace T. and R. E. Plimpton—*Art and Archeology*
Hayward, Arthur H.—*Colonial Lighting*
Higginson, Thomas Wentworth—*Life of Francis Higginson*
Hough, Walter—*Collection of Heating and Lighting Utensils in the United States National Museum* (Bulletin 141 of the U. S. National Museum, Smithsonian Institution)
Langdon, William Chauncy—*Everyday Things in American Life, 1607-1876*
Lindsay, Seymore—*Iron and Brass Implements*

Luchiesh, Mathew—*Torch of Civilization*

McKearin, Helen and George S.—*American Glass*

Mercer, Henry C.—*Light and Fire Making* (Contributions to American History by the Bucks Country Historical Society, No. 4)

Moore, N. Hudson—*Old China Book*

Moore, N. Hudson—*Old Pewter, Brass, Copper and Sheffield Plate*

Norton, C. A. Quincy—*Lights and Lamps of Early New England* (Proceedings, Connecticut Historical Society)

Nutting, Wallace—*Furniture Treasury,* Vol. 2

O' Dea, W. T.—*Social History of Lighting*

Rowson, Marion Nicholl—*Candle Days*

Robins, F. W.—*Story of the Lamp*

Robotti, Frances Diane—*Chronicles of Old Salem*

Roy, L. M. A.—*Candle Book*

Thomas, William Widgery—*Sweden and the Swedes*

Thwing, Leroy—*Flickering Flames*

Thwing, Leroy—*Old Lamps of Central Europe and Other Lighting Devices* (This is a faithful English-language transcription of the Von Benesch book listed below, which includes most of the original plates.)

U. S. National Museum—*Proceedings,* Vol. 3, 1881

Von Benesch, Ladislaus Edler—*Das Beleuchtungswesen*

Walsh, William S.—*Handy Book of Curious Information*

Watkins, C. Malcom—"Artificial Lighting in America, 1830-1860" (In *Report of the Smithsonian Institution,* 1951, Publication no. 4080)

Willison, George F.—*Saints and Strangers*

Williams, W. Mathieu "Oils and Candles" (In *British Manufacturing Industries,* Vol. 4, 1876)

Williamson, Scott Graham—*American Craftsman*

Index

Page references to illustrations are in italics.